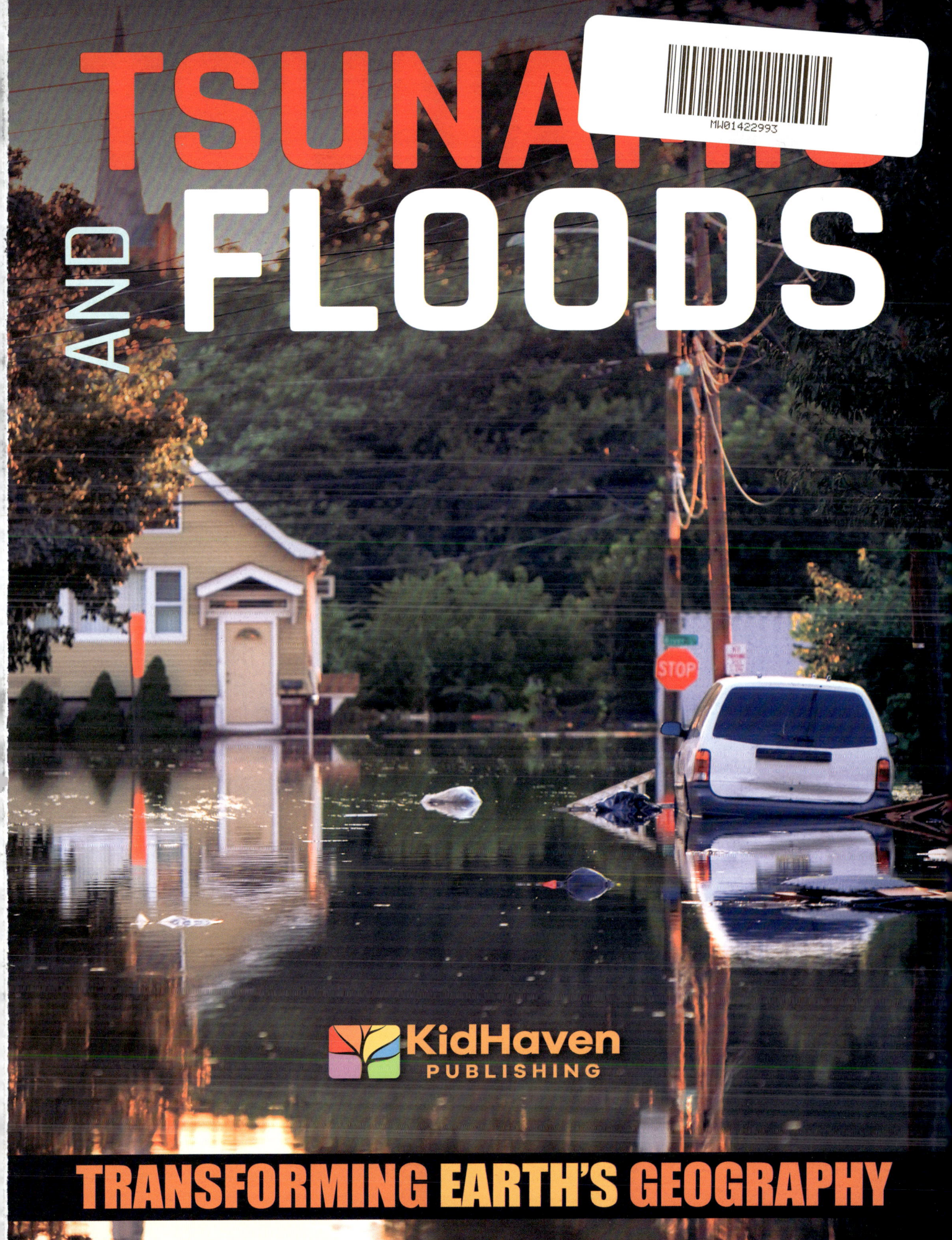

TSUNAMIS AND FLOODS

TRANSFORMING EARTH'S GEOGRAPHY

KidHaven PUBLISHING

Published in 2019 by
KidHaven Publishing, an Imprint of Greenhaven Publishing, LLC
353 3rd Avenue
Suite 255
New York, NY 10010

© 2019 Booklife Publishing
This edition is published by arrangement with Booklife Publishing.

All rights reserved. No part of this book may be reproduced in any form without permission in writing from the publisher, except by a reviewer.

Designer: Gareth Liddington
Editor: Kirsty Holmes

Photo credits: Front Cover & 2 - Bart Sadowski, 4 - mTaira, daulon, 5 - polarman, Mana Photo, 6 - Peter Hermes Furian, Photopictures, 8 - Byelikova Oksana, 9 - Alexyz3d, M. Cornelius, 10 - Yusnizam Yusof, Frans Delian, 11 - Frans Delian, Abdul Razak Latif, mTaira, 12 - Studio BKK, aphichato, 13 - FWStudio, aragami12345s, 14 - Frans Delian, 15 - Frans Delian, 16 - Frans Delian, DoublePHOTO studio, 17 - Frans Delian, michelmond, 18 - Pyty, 19 - mTaira, 20 - Natapat2521, 21 - Cheryl Casey, Matyas Rehak, 22 - Rich Carey, Media Bakery13, 23 - Alexey Seafarer, 24 - Elzbieta Sekowska, Katoosha, 25 - Adalbert Dragon, BABYFRUITY, 26 - Sk Hasan Ali, 27 - Mike Charles, NURWANNA WAEYUSOH, 28 - travelview, FMStox, 29 - David Talukdar, 30 - Sundry Photography, Marc Pinter. Images are courtesy of Shutterstock.com. With thanks to Getty Images, Thinkstock Photo and iStockphoto.

All facts, statistics, web addresses and URLs in this book were verified as valid and accurate at time of writing. No responsibility for any changes to external websites or references can be accepted by either the author or publisher.

Cataloging-in-Publication Data

Names: Brundle, Joanna.
Title: Tsunamis and floods / Joanna Brundle.
Description: New York : KidHaven Publishing, 2019. | Series: Transforming Earth's geography | Includes glossary and index.
Identifiers: ISBN 9781534528994 (pbk.) | ISBN 9781534529014 (library bound) | ISBN 9781534529007 (6 pack) | ISBN 9781534529021 (ebook)
Subjects: LCSH: Tsunamis–Juvenile literature. | Floods–Juvenile literature. | Natural disasters–Juvenile literature.
Classification: LCC GC221.5 B78 2019 | DDC 551.46′37–dc23

Printed in the United States of America

CPSIA compliance information: Batch #BW19KL: For further information contact Greenhaven Publishing LLC, New York, New York at 1-844-317-7404.

Please visit our website, www.greenhavenpublishing.com. For a free color catalog of all our high-quality books, call toll free 1-844-317-7404 or fax 1-844-317-7405.

TSUNAMIS AND FLOODS

CONTENTS

Page 4	What Is a Tsunami?
Page 6	What Causes a Tsunami?
Page 10	Effects of Tsunamis
Page 12	Tsunami Protection
Page 14	Indian Ocean, 2004
Page 18	Japan, 2011
Page 20	What Causes Floods?
Page 24	River Floods
Page 26	Effects of Floods
Page 28	New Orleans, 2005
Page 29	South Asia, 2017
Page 30	Flood Defenses
Page 31	Glossary
Page 32	Index

Words that look like **this** can be found in the glossary on page 31.

WHAT IS A TSUNAMI?

Imagine a peaceful coastline. Maybe you are on the beach or playing in the waves. Suddenly, something strange happens. The sea begins to draw away from the beach, exposing the seafloor. A few minutes later, a giant wave is approaching the beach. It is threatening everything in its path. Run! It's a tsunami.

Deadly, destructive tsunamis are rare. Around the world, on average only two happen each year. Very large, ocean-wide tsunamis are even more uncommon and only happen about once every 10 to 15 years.

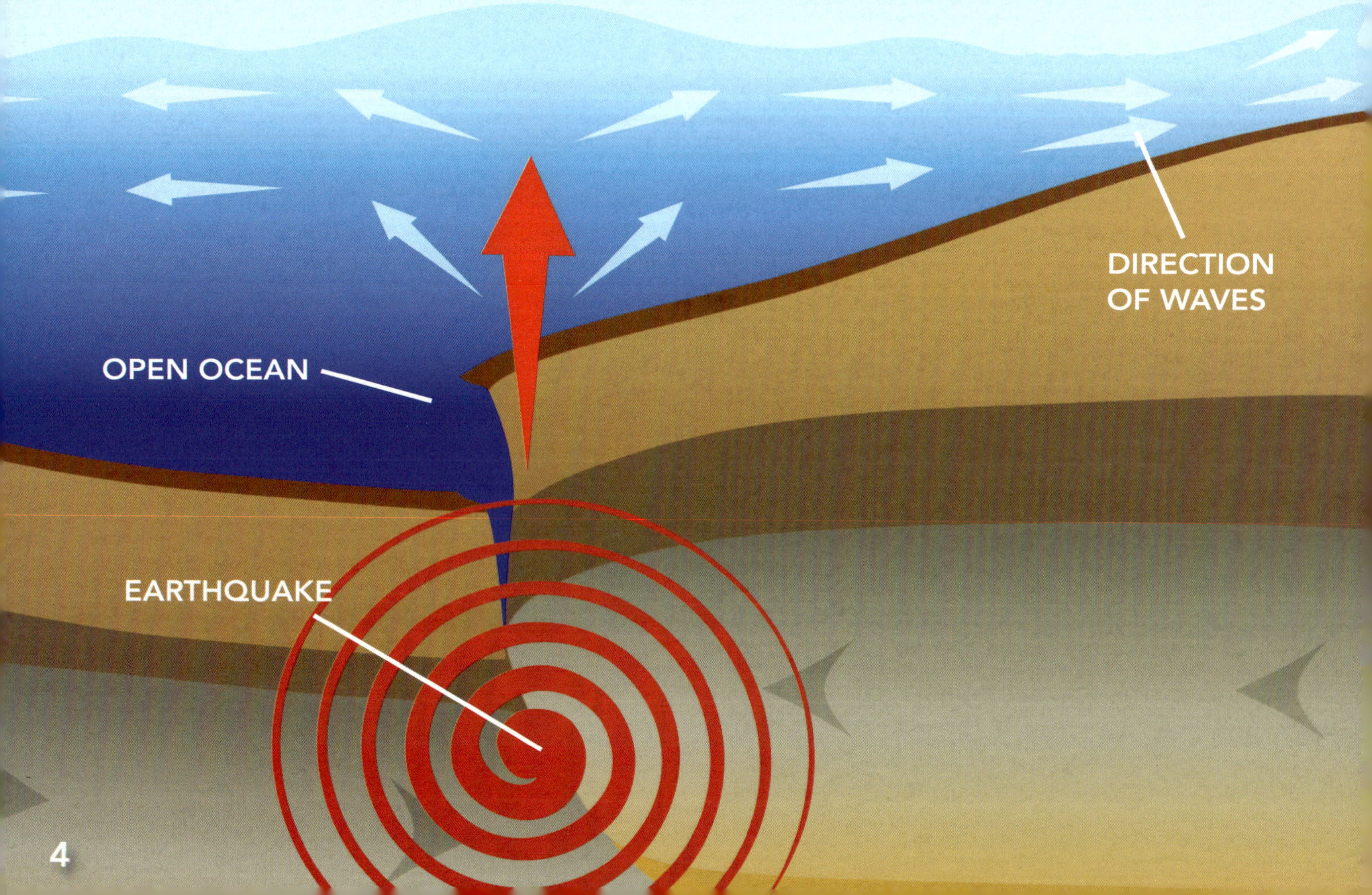

Tsunamis cause total devastation.

DIRECTION OF WAVES

OPEN OCEAN

EARTHQUAKE

A tsunami is a series of waves, often triggered by an earthquake under the seabed. Out at sea, the waves travel quickly, at speeds of up to 500 miles (800 km) per hour. They are low and spread out, and the deeper the water, the faster they travel.

As a wave approaches land, shallower water slows it down. It becomes higher and higher, crashing onto the coast as a towering wall of water. The force of a tsunami wave can sweep away people and property such as cars, boats, and even buildings.

A series of waves, known as a wave train, follows the first wave. There may be a few minutes or up to an hour between the waves.

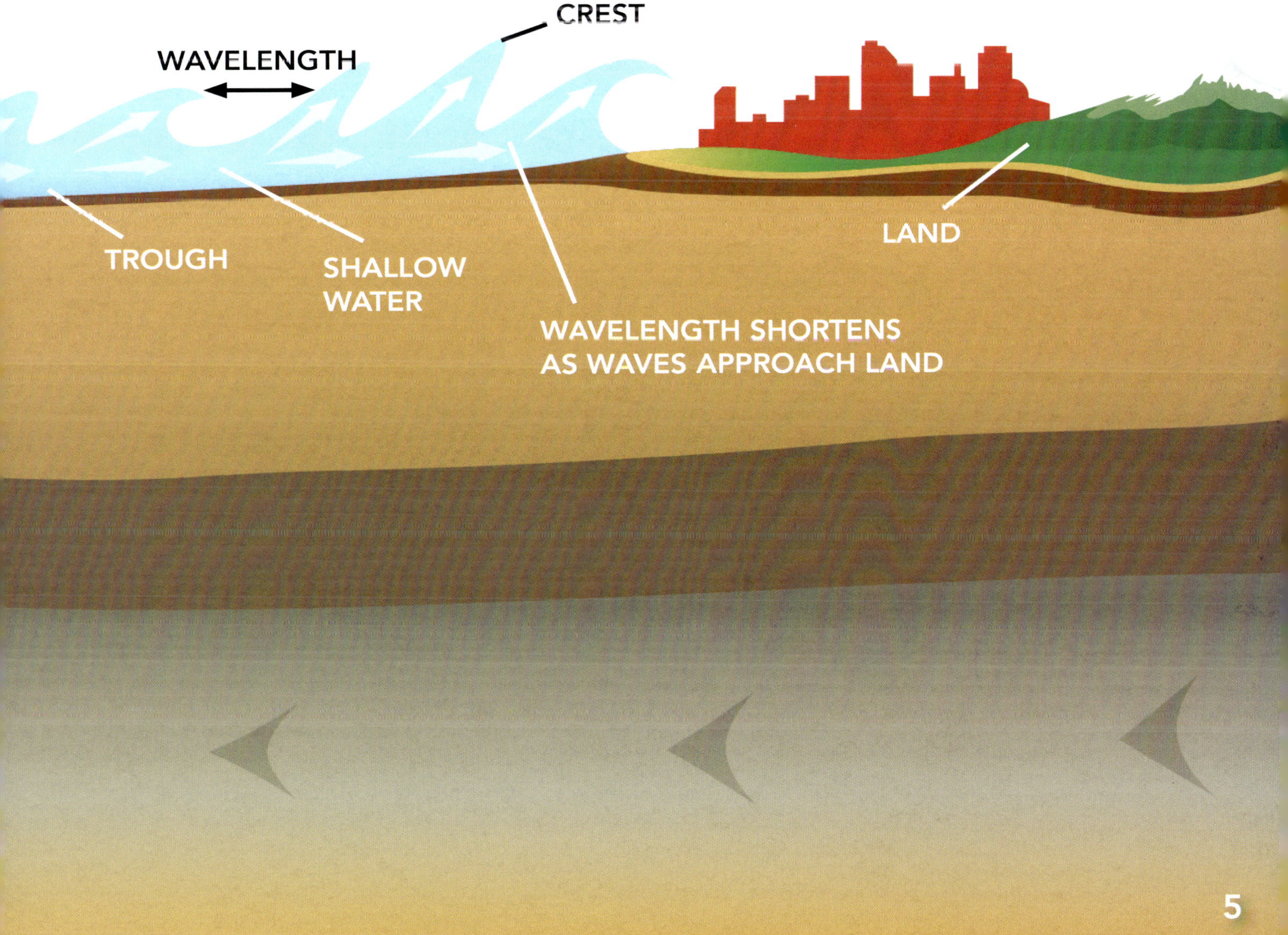

Unlike ordinary waves that break on the shore and flow back, tsunami waves keep moving forwards up to 0.6 miles (1 km) inland, carrying debris with them.

CREST

WAVELENGTH

TROUGH

SHALLOW WATER

WAVELENGTH SHORTENS AS WAVES APPROACH LAND

LAND

5

WHAT CAUSES A TSUNAMI?

EARTHQUAKES

The outer layer of Earth, known as the crust, is made up of huge slabs of rock called tectonic plates. These fit together like a giant jigsaw puzzle. The plates are constantly moving – grinding together, pulling apart, or sliding underneath one another. These movements create a huge pressure that can cause cracks on the Earth's surface, called fault lines. Earthquakes usually happen along these fault lines. Earthquakes that happen under the sea can cause tsunamis.

A Japanese legend claims that earthquakes and tsunamis are triggered by the movements of a giant catfish named Namazu. The word "tsunami" comes from two Japanese words, "tsu" meaning "harbor" and "nami" meaning "wave."

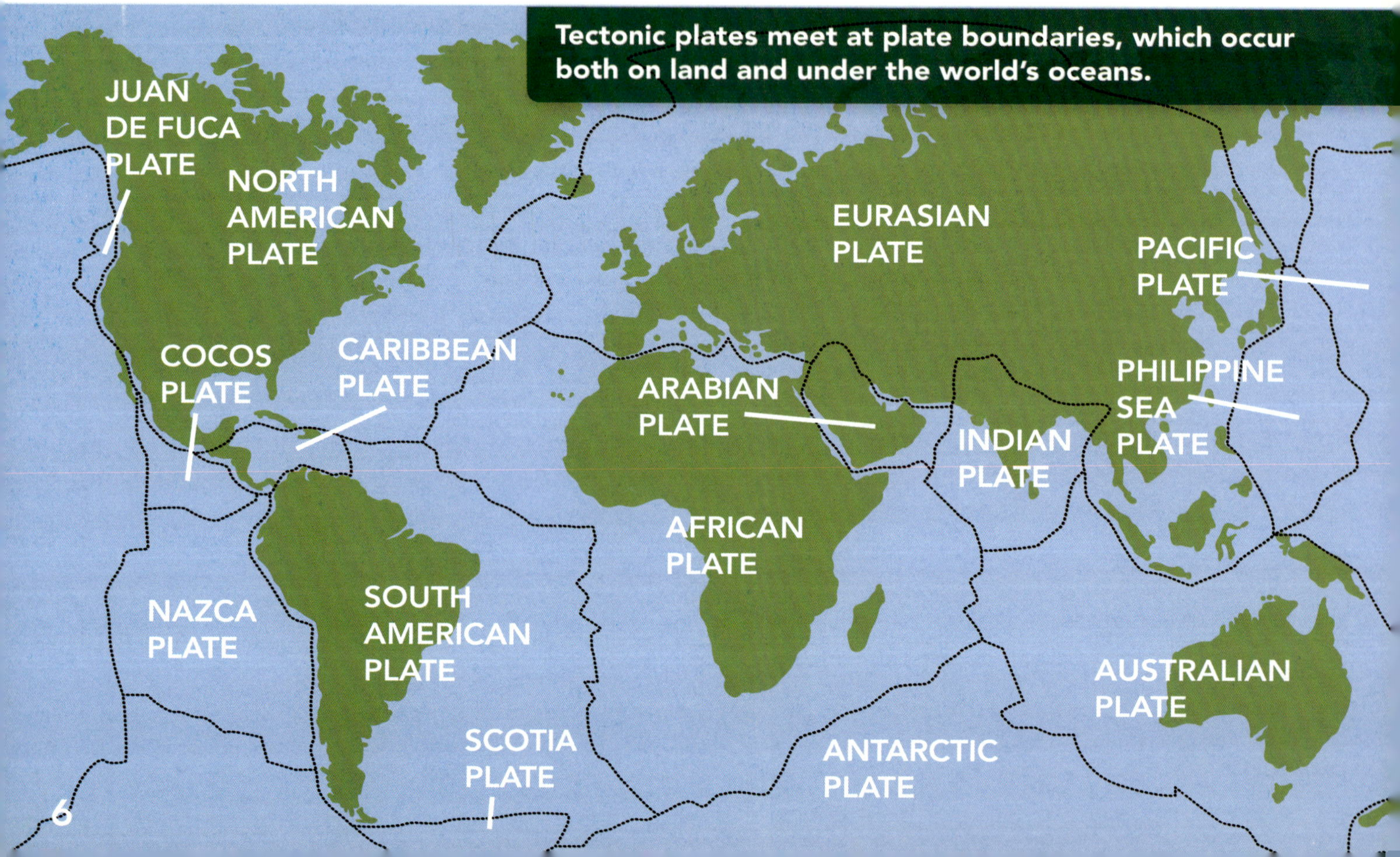

Tectonic plates meet at plate boundaries, which occur both on land and under the world's oceans.

JUAN DE FUCA PLATE
NORTH AMERICAN PLATE
COCOS PLATE
CARIBBEAN PLATE
EURASIAN PLATE
PACIFIC PLATE
ARABIAN PLATE
PHILIPPINE SEA PLATE
INDIAN PLATE
AFRICAN PLATE
NAZCA PLATE
SOUTH AMERICAN PLATE
AUSTRALIAN PLATE
SCOTIA PLATE
ANTARCTIC PLATE

A plate boundary where one plate slides underneath another is called a subduction (say: sub-duck-shun) zone. As they slide, the two plates often become locked together. As the lower plate moves, it drags the upper plate downwards, building pressure.

Eventually, the locked section gives way. The edge of the upper plate springs back upwards, like a jack-in-the-box. When this happens under the sea, it causes the ocean floor to lift suddenly and violently. The water above is pushed upwards, triggering a tsunami.

UPPER PLATE

LOWER PLATE

LOCKED AREA

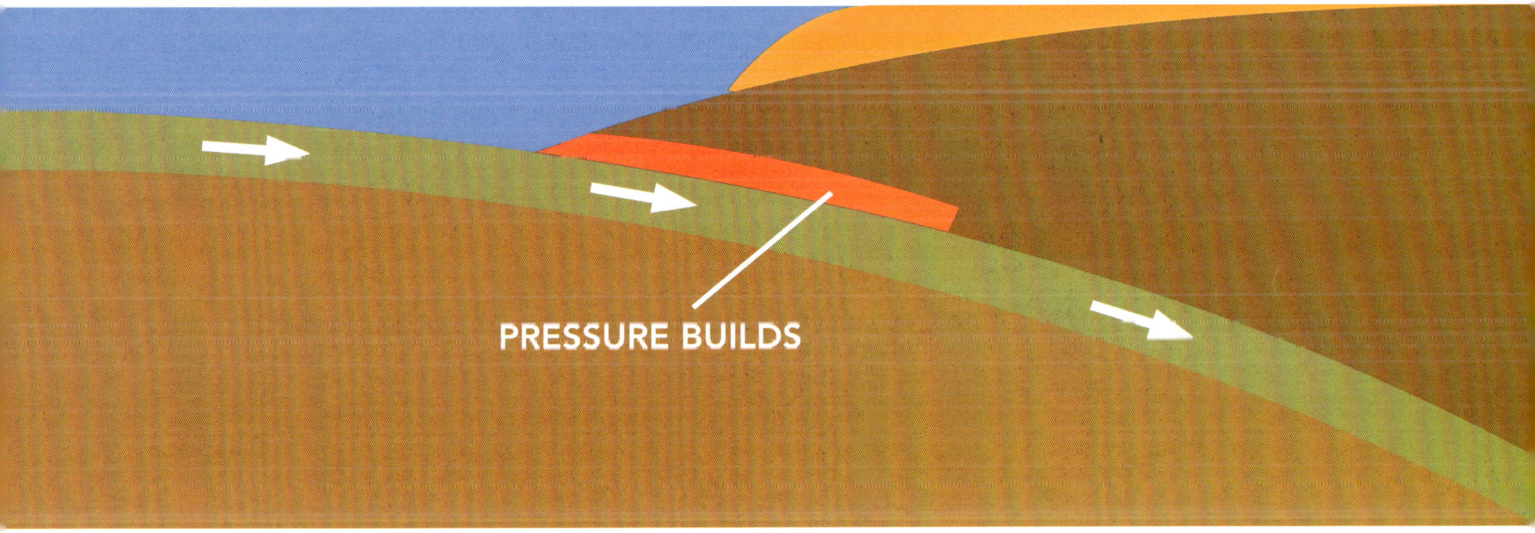

PRESSURE BUILDS

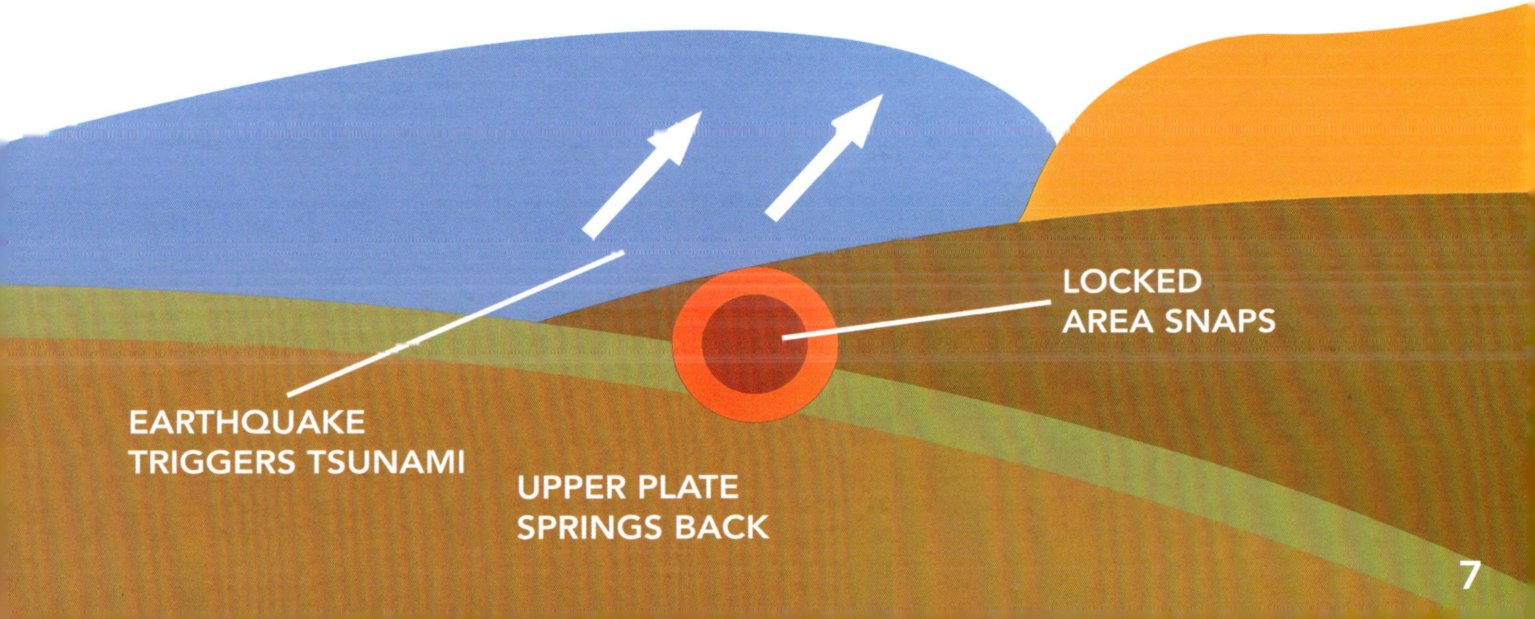

EARTHQUAKE TRIGGERS TSUNAMI

UPPER PLATE SPRINGS BACK

LOCKED AREA SNAPS

VOLCANOES

Submarine (underwater) volcanoes can trigger destructive tsunamis. An erupting submarine volcano can **displace** large amounts of water. It does so by spewing molten rock (lava) into the sea, by exploding, or by collapsing in on itself. Island or coastal volcanoes can also trigger tsunamis by erupting large amounts of volcanic material directly into the sea.

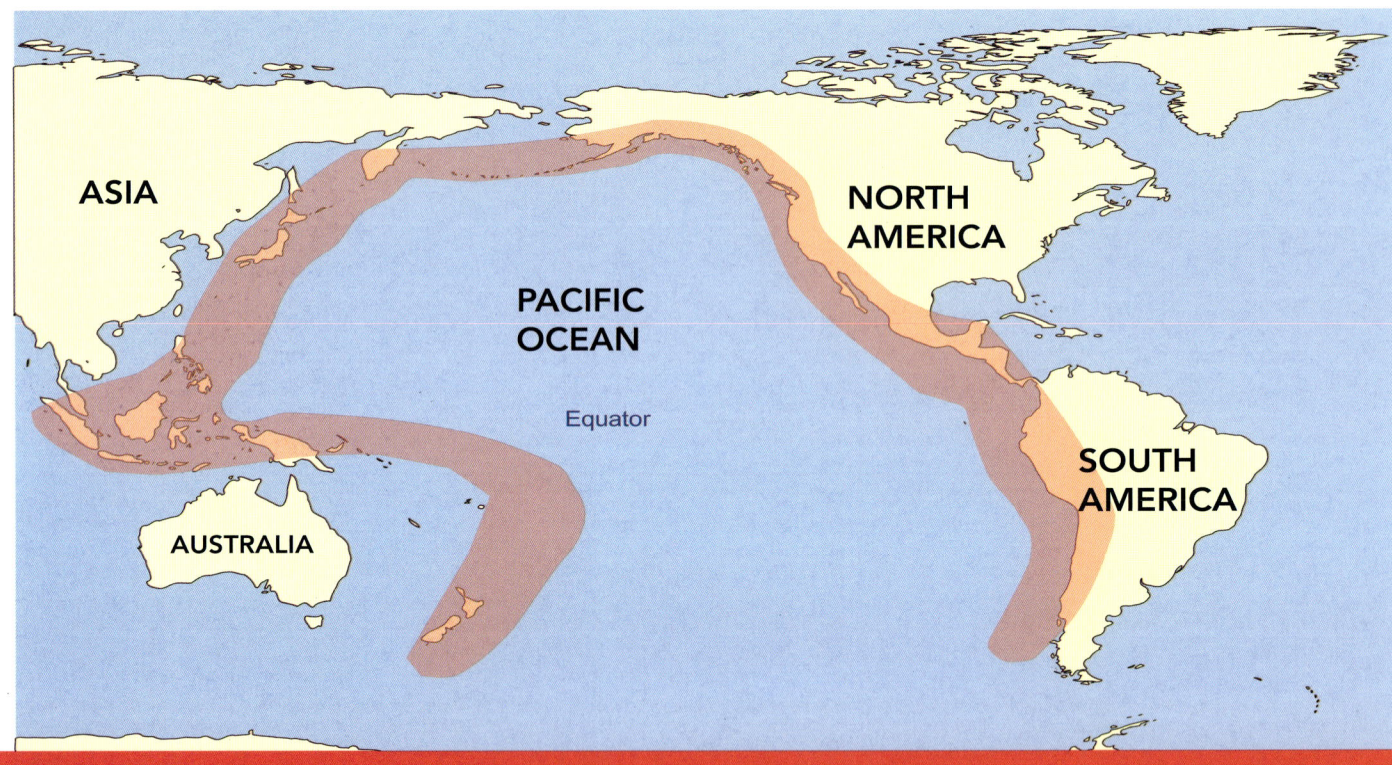

Over 80% of tsunamis happen in the Pacific Ocean. Around its edge are plate boundaries where volcanoes and earthquakes are so common that it is known as the Ring of Fire.

KRAKATOA

In 1883, a volcanic eruption blew apart the Indonesian island of Krakatoa. The explosion and collapse of the volcano into the sea triggered one of the largest and most destructive tsunamis ever recorded. The 130-foot- (40 m) high waves destroyed 165 coastal villages.

Some scientists think that the Minoans, an ancient Greek civilization on the island of Crete, were killed in 1490 BC by a tsunami. It was caused by an erupting volcano in the Aegean Sea.

LANDSLIDES

Tsunamis can be triggered by landslides either under the sea or in coastal areas. In turn, these landslides may be caused by earthquakes. In 1958, an earthquake at Lituya Bay, Alaska, caused a huge landslide into the bay. The tsunami wave it triggered rushed across the bay and reached 1,750 feet (524 m) high on the opposite side.

Lituya Bay, Alaska

The tsunami wave that raced across the bay was the highest ever recorded.

ASTEROIDS

Around 65 million years ago, almost all the dinosaurs on Earth died out. Some scientists believe that a giant asteroid was to blame, crashing into Earth and causing earthquakes, volcanic eruptions, and giant tsunami waves.

Asteroids are rocky objects in space. They orbit the sun but can, very occasionally, crash into the Earth.

EFFECTS OF TSUNAMIS

Tsunamis cause serious flooding. The force of a wall of water moving quickly brings complete devastation. People are killed by drowning or by being struck by collapsing buildings or debris. Many others are injured. Their homes, businesses, and property are destroyed. Only the strongest buildings remain standing.

This tsunami survivor is sitting in the wreckage of his home.

Essential services such as health care, electricity, water supply, transportation, and communications are damaged. Food is hard to find and **contamination** of the water supply can lead to serious diseases.

These bottles are being filled with clean drinking water for tsunami survivors.

In coastal areas, many people earn their living from **tourism** and fishing. After a tsunami, these industries are wiped out.

People Fishing in Indonesia

Tsunamis uproot trees and other vegetation. They destroy animal habitats and food sources. Land animals are killed or injured. Sea creatures may be killed by chemicals or debris washed from the land into the sea.

The force of a tsunami can carry boats from the sea far inland. The tree line shows how far the waves reached.

Communities take a long time to recover. Families may have become separated and unable to communicate with one another. Survivors may suffer long-term injuries or mental health problems.

Tsunamis completely change the appearance of an area. Afterwards, clearing up the mess and rebuilding is a long and expensive process. The dumping and burning of garbage damages the environment even more.

This little girl is trying to comfort her baby sister. They only have the clothes they are wearing – everything else, including their toys, has been destroyed.

Soil may be contaminated by salt from the seawater, making it difficult to grow crops.

Rice Fields in Indonesia

11

TSUNAMI PROTECTION

Most tsunamis happen in the Pacific Ocean. After a tsunami hit Hawaii in 1946, the Pacific Tsunami Warning Center was set up to warn of future disasters. No such system was in place in the Indian Ocean when a deadly earthquake and tsunami struck in 2004 (see pages 14–17). Since then, a network of detectors has also been set up in this region.

THE DART

The DART (Deep-Ocean Assessment and Reporting of Tsunamis) warning system has a sensor that sits on the seabed, measuring the pressure of the water above it. If a tsunami passes, signals are sent to a buoy, floating on the surface. The buoy transmits information to a **satellite**, which sends an alarm to early warning centers on land.

- TSUNAMI WARNING CENTER
- SATELLITE
- TSUNAMI DATA
- PRESSURE SENSOR
- SURFACE BUOY
- SEABED

Loudspeakers broadcast the tsunami warning to everyone in the surrounding area.

STAYING SAFE

If you are in a tsunami zone, listen for warnings. Make sure you know the way inland or to higher ground. **Evacuate** immediately if told to do so.

It is a good idea to keep a lightweight survival kit containing water, food, and a first-aid kit packed, so that you can take it with you if you have to leave in a hurry.

Signs like this warn people that they are in a tsunami zone and direct them to the evacuation route.

WARNING SIGNS

Ground tremors and shakes are signs of an earthquake that could trigger a tsunami. Remember, the sea usually goes out at regular times with the tide. If the sea goes out unexpectedly, it is a sure sign that a tsunami is coming. The trough of the wave following behind acts like a giant vacuum cleaner, sucking the water back from the beach or harbor before the tsunami wave strikes.

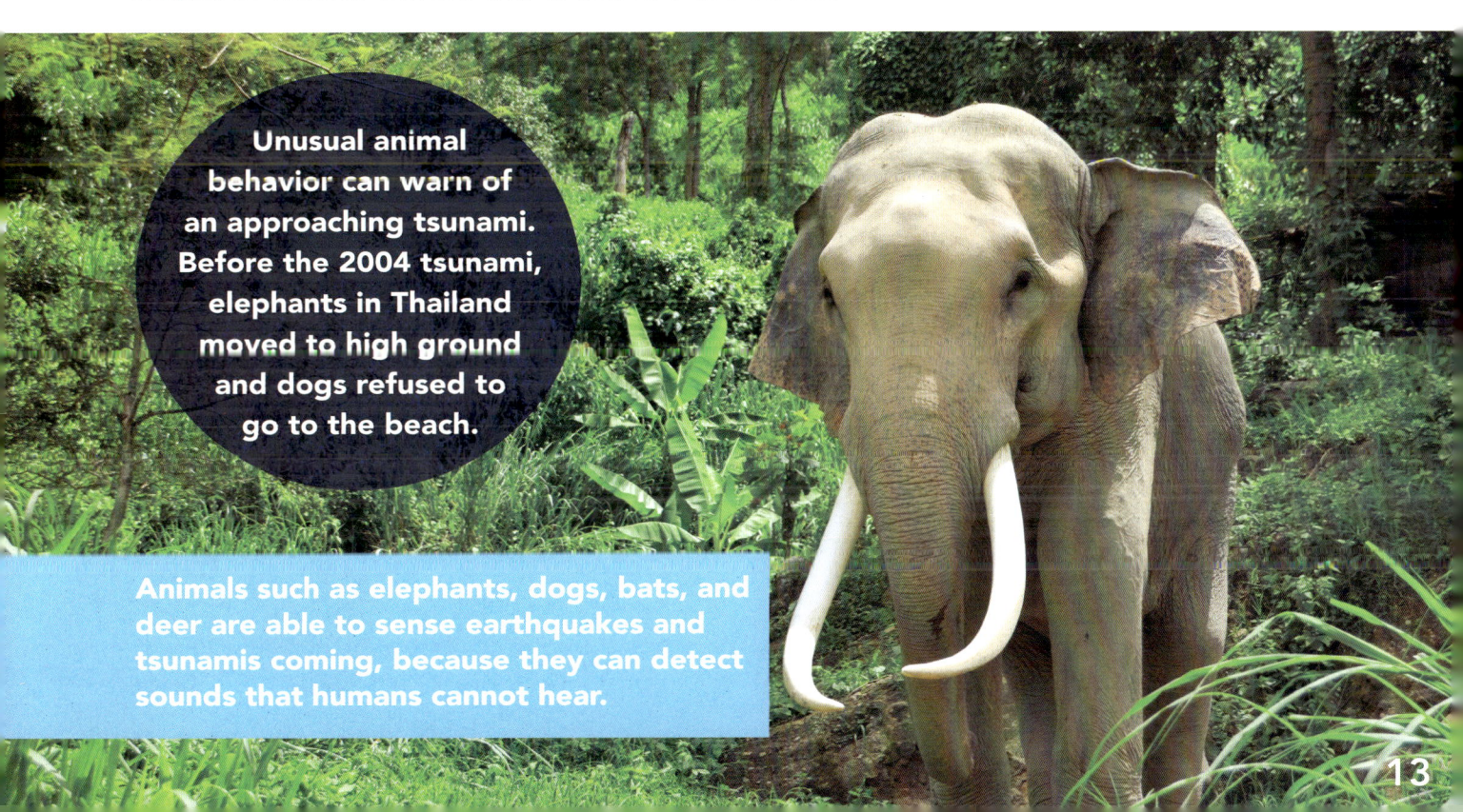

Unusual animal behavior can warn of an approaching tsunami. Before the 2004 tsunami, elephants in Thailand moved to high ground and dogs refused to go to the beach.

Animals such as elephants, dogs, bats, and deer are able to sense earthquakes and tsunamis coming, because they can detect sounds that humans cannot hear.

INDIAN OCEAN, 2004

On the December 26, 2004, one of the most powerful earthquakes ever recorded struck off the coast of the Indonesian island of Sumatra. The earthquake was the result of the Indo-Australian plate sliding underneath, or subducting, below the Eurasian plate. It ripped a gash 930 miles (1,500 km) long in the seabed. The sea floor was violently lifted, triggering tsunami waves that spread out in all directions across the Indian Ocean. The waves traveled at speeds of up to 500 miles (800 km) per hour.

The earthquake measured a massive 9.3 on the Richter scale, which is one of the measures used to show the force of earthquakes. Any measurement over seven is considered a major earthquake.

The earthquake was the longest ever recorded, lasting between eight and ten minutes.

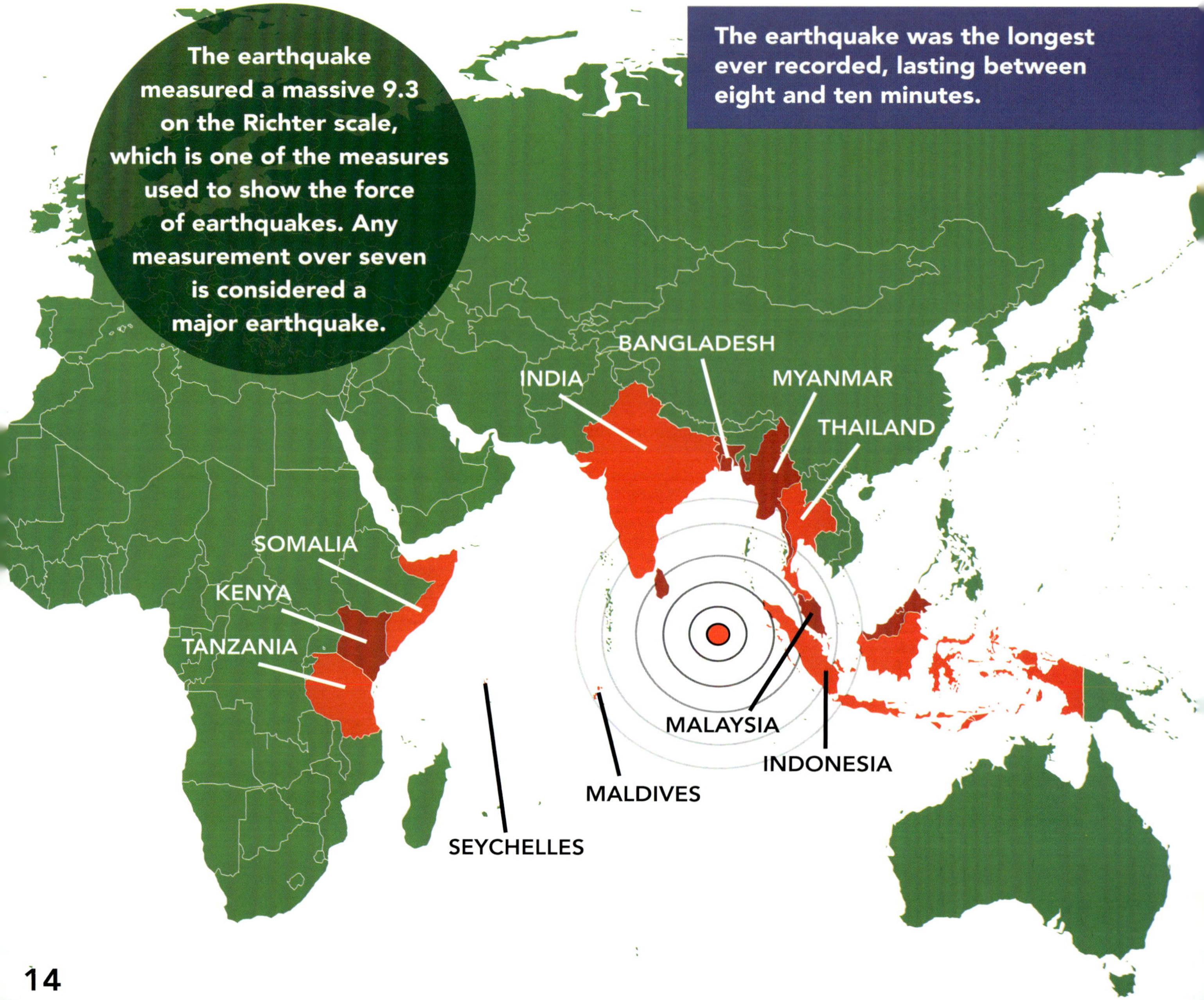

BANGLADESH
INDIA
MYANMAR
THAILAND
SOMALIA
KENYA
TANZANIA
MALAYSIA
INDONESIA
MALDIVES
SEYCHELLES

14

The tsunami waves reached land with huge force, causing total devastation. The **epicenter** of the earthquake was close to **densely populated** coastal areas and no early warning system was in place. People had no time to escape and thousands were killed.

Many tourists on their Christmas vacation wandered out towards the sea, fascinated by the withdrawing ocean and the fish left stranded on the sand. Moments later, they were engulfed by tsunami waves.

The earthquake was felt as far away as Bangladesh, and the tsunami waves reached East Africa and the Pacific Ocean. The total number of people killed was 227,898, making this tsunami the sixth deadliest **natural disaster** in history. Around two million people were made homeless. The total cost of the damage was thought to be ten billion dollars.

The tsunami ripped up roads, so helicopters were used to deliver food and medical supplies to survivors of the disaster.

Any tsunami that travels over 1,000 km is called a teletsunami.

TIMELINE OF THE 2004 TSUNAMI

Tourism, an important source of income for local people, is wiped out.

01:14 GMT
The Pacific Tsunami Warning Center in Hawaii registers the earthquake and sends out a warning.

02:00 GMT
The tsunami hits Burma and Malaysia. An hour has now passed since the earthquake, but victims continue to be caught by surprise because no warning system exists throughout the area.

7:59 a.m. local, **00:59** GMT
The earthquake strikes.

The province of Banda Aceh is worst hit, with over 60% of its buildings destroyed.

01:30 GMT
The tsunami hits the Indonesian island of Sumatra. In some places, waves reach nearly 115 feet (35 m).

02:30 GMT
Reports begin to come in that the south and west coasts of Thailand have been hit by the tsunami. The death toll in this area eventually reaches 5,300 people, many of them tourists.

03:00 GMT
The tsunami hits more than 500 miles (800 km) of the coast of Sri Lanka, destroying homes and tourist areas. More than 30,000 people are killed. Fishing villages and coastal towns in southern India are destroyed. Another 9,000 people are killed here, mostly women and children. People fishing out at sea are able to ride over the wave but return home to find their homes and families destroyed.

07:00 GMT
The tsunami waves hit East Africa, around 4,350 miles (7,000 km) away from the earthquake's epicenter. Around 300 people die in Somalia. In Kenya, people at risk have been evacuated and only one person dies.

December 27th, 2004
Foreign governments and international charities promise emergency aid. Planes carrying food, medical supplies, and relief workers head for the disaster areas.

04:00 GMT
The tsunami washes over the low-lying Maldives. Two thirds of the capital city Male (say: mah-lay) and most of the small islands are flooded.

15:30 GMT
As far away as Mexico and South America, sea levels rise by more than 7 feet.

Throughout the day, the massive scale of the disaster becomes clear. Searches begin to find survivors among the debris. A series of **aftershocks** makes this even more difficult.

JAPAN, 2011

Japan lies in an area where several tectonic plates come together. As a result, earthquakes in the region are common. The earthquake that struck on March 11, 2011, was unusual because of its force. Measuring 9.0 on the Richter scale, it happened 80 miles (130 km) off the coast and pushed the seabed upwards by 23 feet (7 m). The tsunami waves triggered by the earthquake raced to the shore, where waves up to 33 feet (10 m) tall caused total devastation.

The great force of the earthquake moved the main island of Honshu eastwards by over 6 feet (2 m).

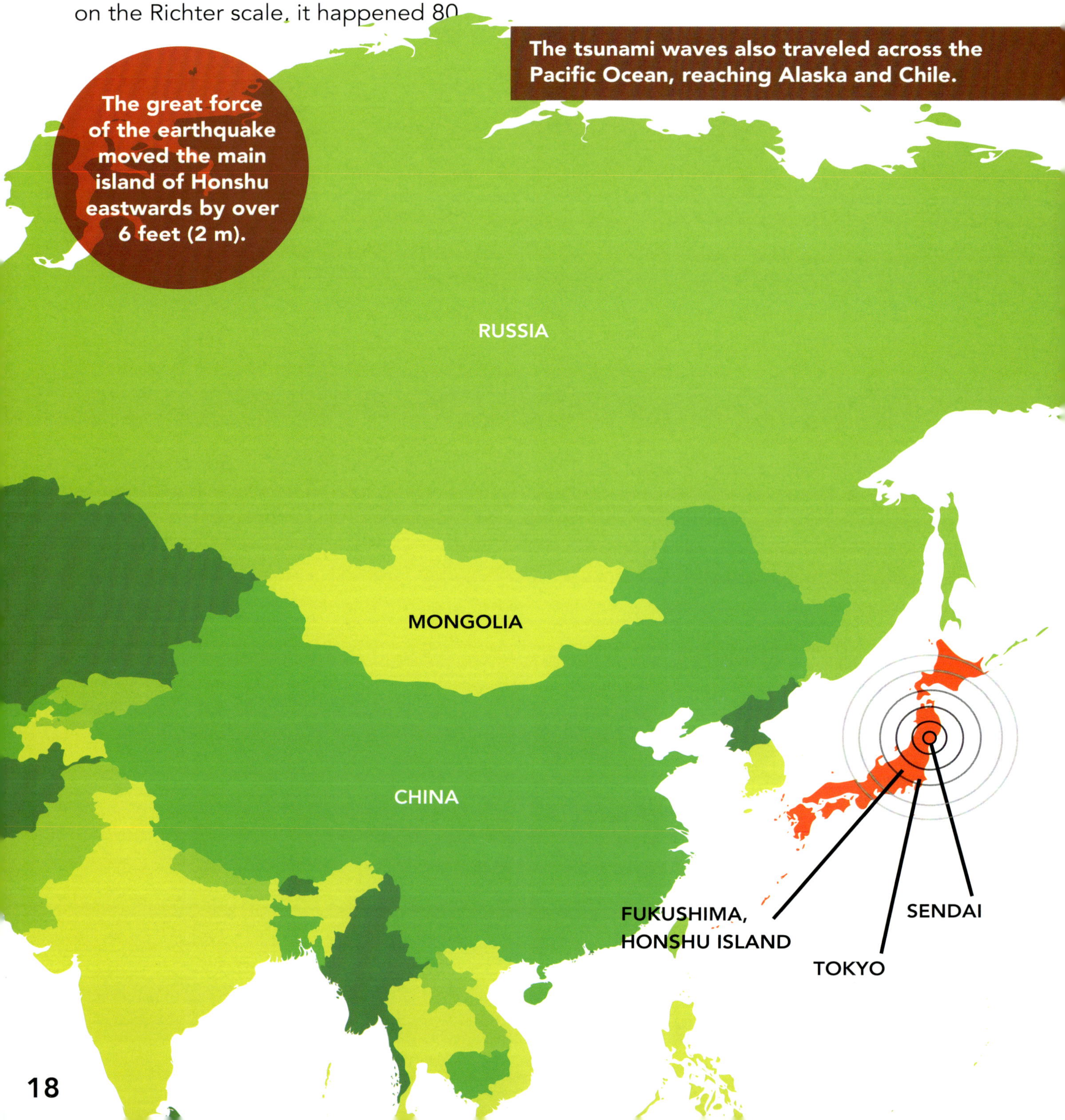

The tsunami waves also traveled across the Pacific Ocean, reaching Alaska and Chile.

RUSSIA

MONGOLIA

CHINA

FUKUSHIMA, HONSHU ISLAND

SENDAI

TOKYO

18

The tsunami destroyed everything in its path.

The tsunami waves rushed inland and caused damage around 130 feet (40 m) above normal sea level. An area of 215 square miles (560 sq km) was flooded. When the water eventually flowed back to sea, millions of tons of debris were washed out into the ocean. Some of this is still being washed up as far away as the coast of the United States.

The force of the tsunami was enough to knock over houses and carry boats and cars inland.

The tsunami also caused a disaster at the Fukushima **nuclear plant**. Explosions, triggered by tsunami damage to the cooling systems, led to leaks of harmful **radioactive** material into the air. Around 300,000 people had to be evacuated at the time and the area remains unsafe.

WHAT CAUSES FLOODS?

Floods can be caused by meltwater (water from melting snow and ice) or by heavy, prolonged rainfall. Rain normally soaks away into the ground or runs off the ground into **watercourses**. If the ground cannot soak up any more water, it is said to be saturated. The extra water then floods onto flat land or fills watercourses until they overflow.

The water table is an imaginary line beneath Earth's surface. Under the line, the ground is saturated. Above the line, the ground can absorb more water. Heavy rain can raise the water table, causing surface floods.

THUNDERSTORMS AND MICROBURSTS

Microbursts result in high winds as well as very heavy rain as they hit the ground.

Thunderstorms form when warm, moist air rises rapidly over land or sea. As the water vapor cools, it builds towering thunderclouds, which drop large amounts of rainfall. Small columns of fast-sinking air and rain and hail called wet microbursts form in thunderstorms.

Thunderstorms and microbursts, like this dramatic example in Bangkok, Thailand, often cause flooding.

COASTAL FLOODING

Very high tides can also cause flooding, especially if they happen at the same time as storm surges.

Coastal flooding happens when the level of the sea rises. Seawater flows into low-lying areas that are normally dry, causing flooding. As we have seen, coastal flooding can be caused by tsunamis. Storm surges are sudden rises in sea level, caused by storms, hurricanes, and tropical cyclones. Heavy rain falls and strong winds push up the water on the surface of the ocean, piling up the water and increasing the sea level.

A hurricane has caused coastal flooding along this seafront.

MONSOON RAINS

In 2010, heavy monsoon rains in Pakistan led to devastating floods that made 1.7 million people homeless and left 20% of the country underwater.

A monsoon is a wind that changes direction with the seasons. During the summer monsoon, winds pick up moisture from the sea. They are pulled inland by the warm land, where they drop the moisture as torrential rains. The ground becomes saturated and rivers overflow.

Monsoon rains have flooded this market in India.

21

HUMAN CAUSES

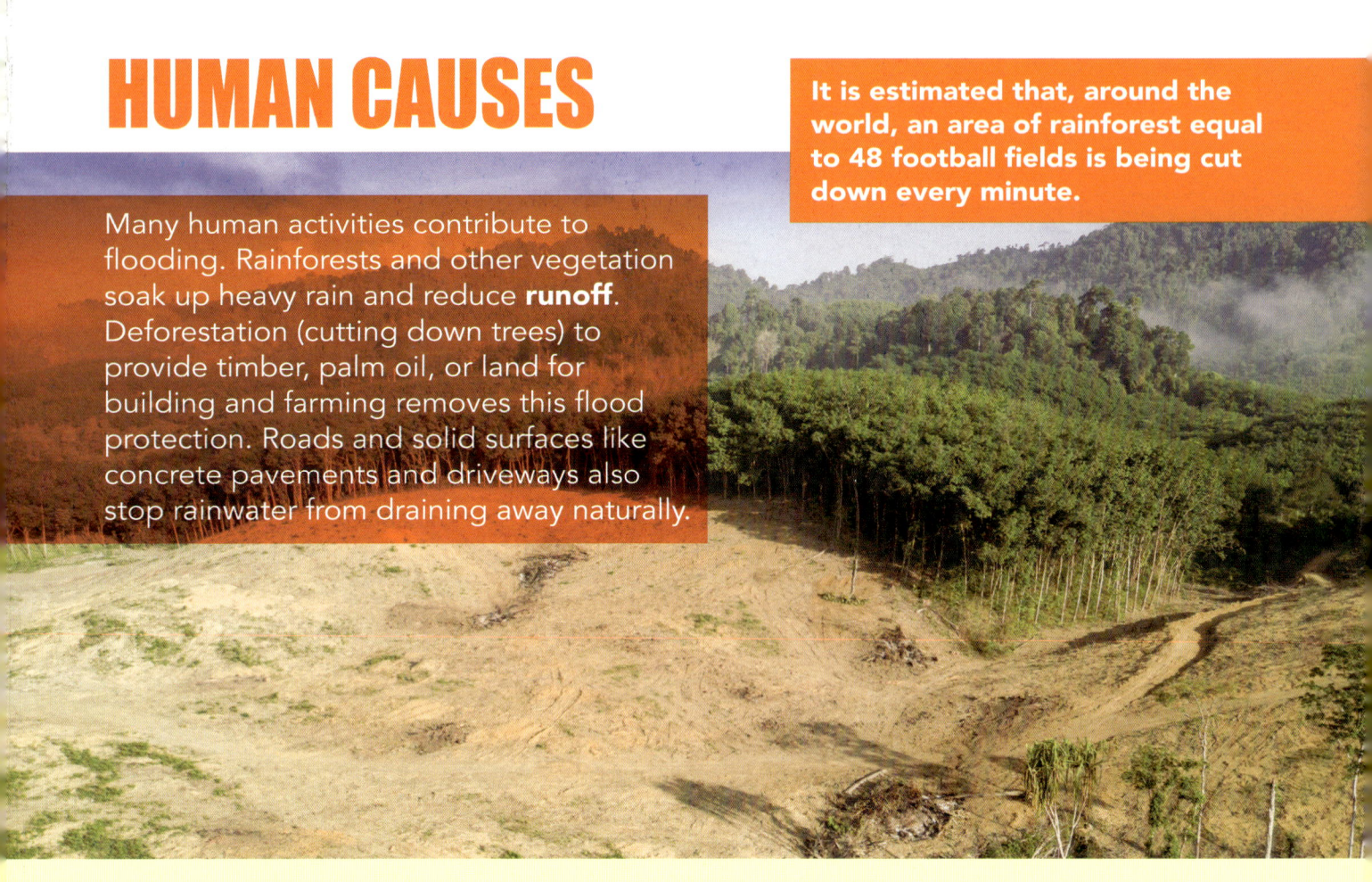

It is estimated that, around the world, an area of rainforest equal to 48 football fields is being cut down every minute.

Many human activities contribute to flooding. Rainforests and other vegetation soak up heavy rain and reduce **runoff**. Deforestation (cutting down trees) to provide timber, palm oil, or land for building and farming removes this flood protection. Roads and solid surfaces like concrete pavements and driveways also stop rainwater from draining away naturally.

WILDFIRES

Floods often follow **wildfires**. Wildfires destroy vegetation and leave the surface of the ground charred and unable to absorb rainwater. Flooding after wildfires is often particularly dangerous. Ash and other debris combine with rainwater to form mudslides, which cause serious damage.

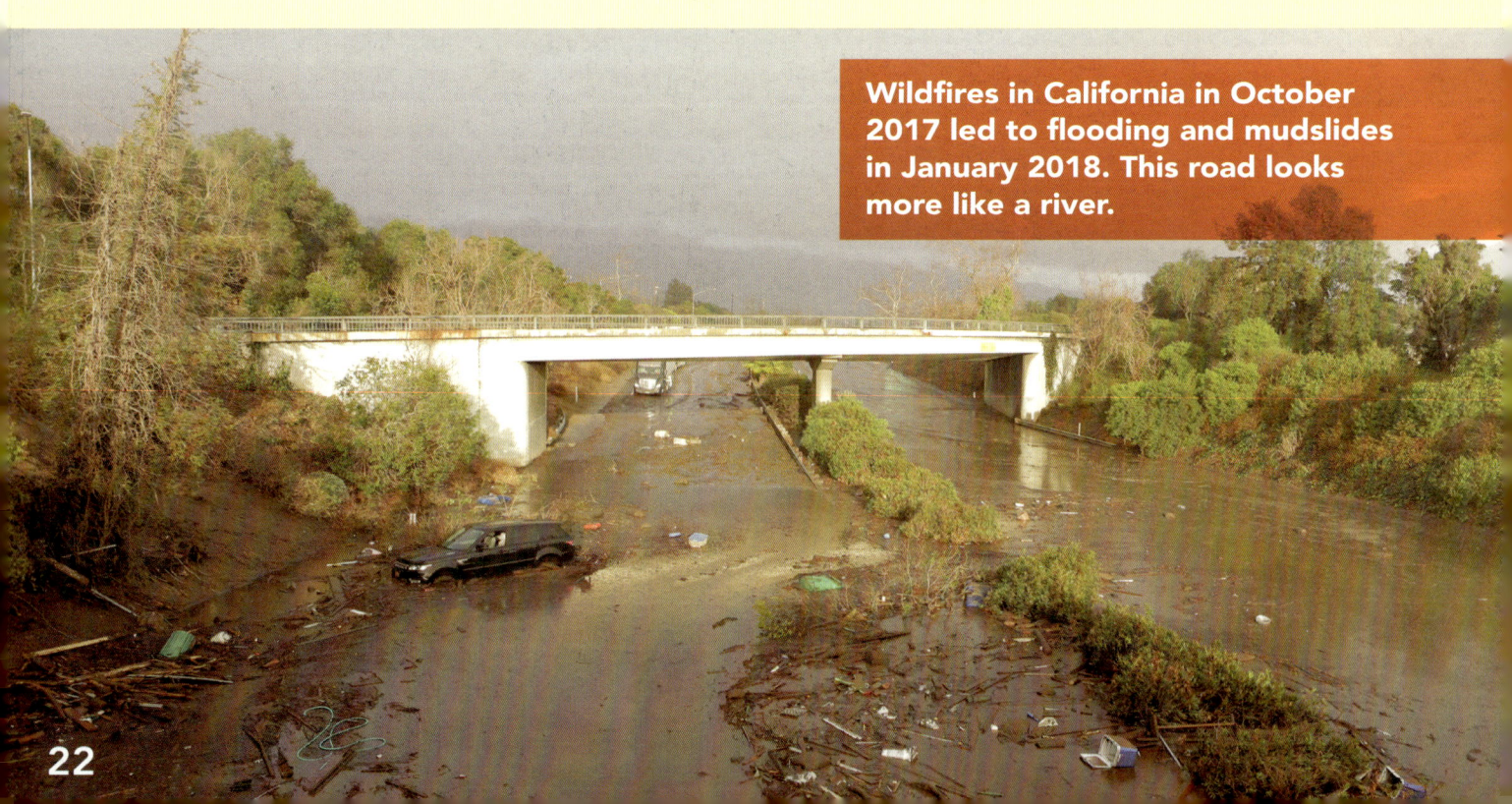

Wildfires in California in October 2017 led to flooding and mudslides in January 2018. This road looks more like a river.

Global warming is melting ice caps in the Arctic and Antarctica.

GLOBAL WARMING

Global warming is also causing droughts in areas that used to receive regular rainfall.

Humans burn **fossil fuels** such as coal and oil to provide energy. As they burn, fossil fuels release carbon dioxide and other gases, known as greenhouse gases. These gases trap heat from the sun – just like a greenhouse. Most scientists agree that, as a result, Earth is gradually heating up. This effect is called global warming or climate change. Warmer temperatures are melting the polar ice sheets. This is causing sea levels to rise, increasing the chance of coastal flooding during storms and hurricanes. Devastating, deadly river and monsoon floods, caused by heavy rain, are happening more often.

Scientists think that by the year 2100, sea levels will have risen by 3 feet (1 m) due to global warming. This would cause disastrous coastal flooding and would leave millions of people homeless.

RIVER FLOODS

River flooding, also known as fluvial or overbank flooding, happens when the water level rises over the top of river banks. It can happen in any size of watercourse, from a tiny stream to a mighty river. River floods can be caused by meltwater, as well as by heavy rainfall.

The Huang He (Yellow River) has been nicknamed "China's Sorrow" because its floods have killed millions of people, more than any other river in the world.

BENEFITS OF RIVER FLOODING

Fertile floodplains along the Nile River are used for growing crops and rearing livestock.

Despite the risks, millions of people around the world choose to live on **floodplains**. The **silt** left behind by flood waters makes the soil good for growing crops. Floodwater can be saved and used for irrigation (watering crops) throughout the year.

The Nile River, Egypt

FLASH FLOODS

Flash floods are a type of river flood. They are one of the most dangerous types of flood because they happen very quickly, with little or no warning. They are often caused by slow-moving thunderstorms that drop exceptionally heavy rainfall onto a small area, such as a river valley. Water levels rise rapidly and create a raging flow of water. Steep, narrow rivers act like a funnel for the water. Densely populated areas are at high risk from flash floods. Buildings and roads increase runoff because heavy rainfall cannot easily drain away.

Flash floods in desert areas can turn a dry canyon or riverbed into a fast-flowing torrent of water in minutes.

Flash Floods

Antelope Canyon, Arizona, USA

Flash floods have carved out the sweeping lines of Antelope Canyon over thousands of years.

25

EFFECTS OF FLOODS

Flooding kills approximately 20,000 people around the world every year. People drown in the floods or die from starvation and serious diseases carried in the water. Many more are injured by debris carried in floodwaters. Natural disasters, such as flooding, affect people living in poor areas more than those living in wealthier areas. Their homes may be built of cheap, flimsy materials that are easily washed away. They also lack resources, like money to help them rebuild or transportation, to help them evacuate quickly.

These children in India are having fun on a homemade raft, but floodwaters can carry deadly diseases.

THE FUTURE

The world population is growing. This means that in the future there will be increasing competition for resources, including land. More people will be affected by flooding because they will be forced to live in flood-prone areas. Global warming will add to the problems.

The current population of the world is 7.6 billion, but it is expected to reach 9.7 billion by 2050.

BOSCASTLE, UK

The River Valency that runs through Boscastle has now been lowered and widened to help prevent future flooding.

Boscastle in Cornwall, UK, lies where three small, steep rivers meet. The surrounding hillsides include areas of slate, a rock that cannot absorb rainwater. In August 2004, rainfall for a typical month fell in just two hours onto ground that was already saturated because of recent thunderstorms. Flash floods tore through Boscastle and damaged homes and businesses. They uprooted trees and swept cars, trailers, and other property into the harbor. Helicopters had to be used to rescue around 100 people clinging to roofs and treetops.

Boscastle, UK

27

NEW ORLEANS, 2005

In August 2005, an extremely powerful hurricane in the Gulf of Mexico reached land, causing storm surges up to 33 feet (10 m) high. New Orleans, Louisiana, was one of the areas worst affected by the hurricane, named Katrina, because it lies partly below sea level. **Levees** normally protect the city from flooding from the Mississippi River and Lake Pontchartrain, but they were overwhelmed by the storm surge. Water poured in, flooding over three-quarters of the city. Despite an order to evacuate, many people stayed behind. Around 1,800 people died, many of them too elderly or sick to leave.

Tourism in New Orleans has now recovered. Tourism there provides over 80,000 jobs.

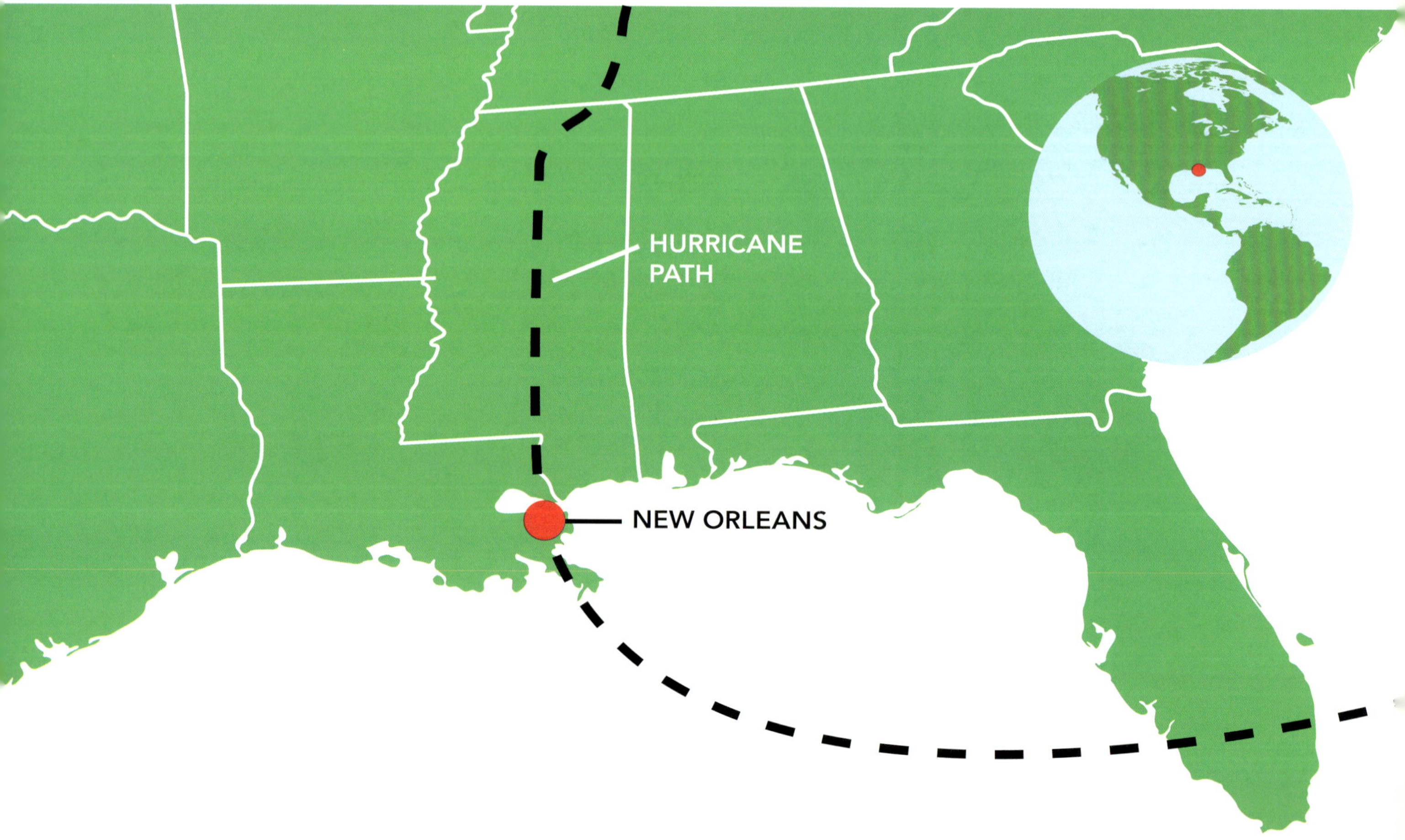

HURRICANE PATH

NEW ORLEANS

SOUTH ASIA, 2017

Severe summer monsoon rains caused serious flooding and landslides across South Asia in 2017. In Nepal, the flooded areas were in the poorest parts of the country, where people live in bare mud homes and rely on their small farms for food. The floods washed away or damaged over 230,000 homes, and farms were left underwater.

These children in India are making their way to school on foot, wading through the floodwater.

Bangladesh is a low-lying and densely populated country. Flooding is common, but the 2017 floods were exceptional. Livestock and crops, including rice, were badly damaged, leading to food shortages and higher prices.

It is estimated that 41 million people in India, Nepal, and Bangladesh were affected by the floods, with many of them being made homeless.

These children have managed to save their family's goat from drowning by building a makeshift boat from banana plants.

FLOOD DEFENSES

Embankments can form naturally or be built up from soil and rocks, covered with grass or concrete.

Walls or embankments may be built along riverbanks. They prevent the river from bursting its banks and overflowing onto the floodplain. Seawalls give protection against high tides and storm surges.

We can help to prevent flooding by building away from floodplains and by using materials for paved areas that allow rainwater to drain away naturally.

The Thames Barrier is one of the largest in the world and protects London from flooding.

London, UK

We can tackle global warming by reducing the amount of fossil fuels we burn. It is the most important thing we can do to protect ourselves against disastrous flooding in the future.

Barrages or barriers are man-made structures built across a river to prevent flooding. Gates in a barrage allow river water to flow normally out to sea, but they can be closed to stop storm surges or high tides from flooding low-lying areas upstream.

GLOSSARY

aftershocks	smaller tremors that happen after the main shock of an earthquake
contamination	the poisoning or pollution of a substance
crops	plants that are grown on a large scale because they are useful, usually as food
debris	the remains of something that has been destroyed
densely populated	having many people living in a small area
displace	move something from its usual place
environment	the natural world
epicenter	the point on Earth's surface which is directly above the focus of the earthquake
evacuate	move away from an area to escape danger
floodplains	areas of low-lying, flat land alongside rivers or streams that are prone to flooding
fossil fuels	fuels, such as coal, oil and gas, that formed millions of years ago from the remains of animals and plants
GMT	(Greenwich Mean Time) the basis of standard time throughout the world, used as a standard for setting different time zones
habitats	the natural environments in which animals or plants live
levees	banks built alongside a river to prevent flooding
natural disaster	a violent natural event that kills or injures people and damages property and the environment
nuclear plant	a power station that produces electricity using nuclear fuels such as uranium
radioactive	giving off a harmful type of energy called radiation
runoff	rainfall or meltwater that runs over the surface of the ground without soaking into it
satellite	a machine in space that orbits planets, takes photographs, and collects and transmits information
silt	a substance made up of sand, clay, and other materials, carried by a river
tourism	the action of visiting places for pleasure and the industry that supports this action
watercourses	bodies of water, such as rivers, streams, or lakes
wildfires	large, destructive fires that burn in areas of vegetation such as woodlands

INDEX

A
asteroids 9

B
barrages 30

C
climate change 23

D
dinosaurs 9
diseases 10, 26

E
earthquakes 4–5, 8–9, 12–18
environment 11

F
fault lines 6
fishing 10, 17
floodplains 24, 30
floods
- coastal 21, 23
- flash 25, 27
- fluvial 24

G
global warming 23, 26, 30

H
habitats 11
hurricanes 21, 23, 28

L
landslides 9, 29
levees 28

M
meltwater 20, 24
microbursts 20
monsoons 21, 23, 29
mudslides 22

O
ocean
- Indian 12, 14–15
- Pacific 8, 12, 15, 18

P
plate boundaries 6–8

R
rainfall 20, 23–25, 27
Ring of Fire 8
rivers 21–25, 27–28, 30
runoff 22, 25

S
seabed 5, 12, 14, 18
storm surges 21, 28, 30
subduction zones 7, 14

T
tectonic plates 6, 18
teletsunamis 15
thunderstorms 20, 25, 27
tourism 10, 16, 28

V
volcanoes 8

W
water tables 20
watercourses 20, 24
wave trains 5
wavelengths 5
waves 4–6, 8–9, 11, 13–15, 17–19